THE
EXECUTIVE
ALLEY

Evolution of the Woman Executive

THE EXECUTIVE ALLEY

Evolution of the Woman Executive

A Woman's Guide to the Top
Through Successful Competition
and the Art of Leadership

LINDA WHEELER

HARA PUBLISHING

This book is the first of a three-part series on the subject of competition between women in the workforce. Book two will present in-depth interviews with successful women and their experiences dealing with competition between women and men. Book three will analyze how our children compete now that society is more inclusive of women as role-models.

Published by Hara Publishing
P.O. Box 19732
Seattle, Washington 98109
(425) 775-7868

Editor: Victoria McCown
Cover Design: Graphic Concepts, Inc.
Book Design: Communication by Design

ISBN 1-883697-99-9

*This book is dedicated
to my daughter, Jamielyn.*

*The most interesting thing about Women in Power is
that those secrets of leadership can be taught. And if
they're taught early enough, they can result in
greater representation of women in political office
and leadership.*
—Geraldine Ferraro, former New York
    Congresswoman and Vice Presidential Candidate

Acknowledgements

I would like to extend my thanks to my husband James, my daughter Jamielyn, and my son Donnico Johnson, whom I love very dearly. They are the foundation on which I have built these dreams. And to my parents George and Leola Hall who are the rock of my heritage.

I would also like to give special thanks to family members and friends who supported me and this project, and trusted in my ability to make it a reality: Dr. Joseph Bell, William Hodge, Jack Graham, Barbara Miller, Brad Brezlin, Sandra Faye Mitchell, Diane and Victor Palmason, Guinda and Alana Clayton, George Hall, Brinda, Sharina, and Gregory Jordan, and Rinda and Jeff Norris. Their support has made a great contribution to this book.

Great things happen when you bring great talent to the table. I would like to give special thanks to:

Dr. Ronald Heifetz, my Leadership Professor whose theory he so graciously allowed me to use. Thank you for the encouragement and support.

Les Brown: Thank you for helping me believe in myself. You are my inspiration.

Rafael Colón, the trail blazer, my friend and confidant. Thank you for your tenacious drive and willingness to help others around you. You have been my coach, mentor, and friend.

Sheryn Hara: My publisher, thank you for everything, without you this would not be.

Lenore Doyle: Your creative mind has been a true blessing, your patience is a virtue, thanks for waiting for me to catch up.

Vicki McCown: My friend and editor, thanks for steering me in the right direction.

Contents

We cannot escape fear. We can only transform it into a companion that accompanies us on all our exciting adventures... Take a risk a day — one small or bold stroke that will make you feel great once you have done it.
—Susan Jeffers

Prologue

Any woman who dares to embark upon the road to becoming a leader must be prepared for a challenge. As women in leadership positions, we will be tested — by our staff, by other department heads, by our superiors, and even by the press. It is a fact of life that women must work harder and overcome more obstacles than their male counterparts to succeed in influential positions. Women must prove themselves to be effective and credible time and time again.

Women in key leadership positions must have all the same skills that men need to be good leaders: the ability to give direction clearly, to be a team player, and to build solid working relationships. But women leaders must also demonstrate that they are trustworthy, meaning that their working relationships are based on integrity and mutual respect. They must know how to lead in the truest sense of the word.

Therefore, before women can lead, they must learn to compete with integrity and respect, for learning to do so is vital to the longevity of their careers as leaders.

*Remember no one makes it alone. Have a grateful heart
and be quick to acknowledge those who help you.*
—Author unknown

We've Come a Long Way, Baby

Although this rallying cry of the feminist movement is now a cliché, it still rings true. As we approach the millennium, women are breaking down barriers in business and industry like never before. With each wave of women who enter the workforce, we are more educated and experienced than our foremothers, faced with a horizon of unlimited opportunities that are ours to seize.

I know, because I'm one of those women who started from the bottom and reached unimaginable heights. And if you're reading this book, chances are you're climbing up that same ladder. But I'm here to tell you that before we women can be truly capable and independent and unstoppable in our achievements, we still have an important lesson to learn: How to compete in the workplace fairly, impersonally, and without fear and anger.

Unfortunately, even though we have evolved from dependent stay-at-home women into independent out-in-the-workforce women, our evolution is not complete. We still need to hone a few skills, most notably how to put our own best foot forward without stepping on the backs of other women.

In this book I will outline strategies women can use to position themselves for future leadership positions. By competing with self-respect and dignity, and arming ourselves with a new knowledge base of leadership skills, women can ensure a successful future and an increase in our number at the highest levels.

I'm going to begin by bringing right out into the open some of the unethical and self-defeating behavior women employ to claw their way to success. I believe that if we expose this behavior, and recognize that women undermining other women is injurious to all of us, then we can learn how to compete in ways that continue to move us forward toward parity with our male counterparts.

This is a controversial subject. Let's face it — many feminists will deny that this problem exists, no doubt afraid to wash our dirty laundry in public. But I know firsthand about the nasty, calculating, devious ways in which women may treat their colleagues and competitors; not only was I the victim of such conduct, I gave as good as I got, feeling I had to engage in the same kind of back-stabbing behavior or be left in the dust. It is just this kind of vindictive, fear-based attitude that I'm hoping to help eradicate. But that will never happen until we first admit that it truly does exist.

Once we learn how to compete, I believe we will become better leaders, which is not only important for ourselves today, but especially significant for those women — our daughters and granddaughters — who will come after us. I will examine some of the strategies we can use to make us leaders worth following.

How It All Began

When I was growing up, my parents never encouraged me to participate in sports or any other competitive activity. "You are a girl," my mother would tell me. "You must act like a lady and remember your manners. You want people to like you." She dressed me and my sisters in lace and bows and sent us off to piano and singing lessons. I daydreamed about growing up to be Cinderella, falling in love and marrying my "prince," and then living happily ever after.

The message my brother got was quite different. He played sports and was encouraged to do whatever he could to win. But with these freedoms came heavy responsibilities. When he turned eighteen, he was considered a man, expected to get out in the world and make his own way.

I think my upbringing was typical of the times, and as I look back now I can see clearly that the ways in which boys and girls developed were quite different: Boys were given opportunities to learn how to compete, to become self-reliant, to dream of greatness. Girls were taught to be "good," to be "likable," all the better to snare a good husband, the inevitable measure of our worth. As future wives and mothers, our goals were to be loving, sensitive, compassionate, and nurturing — traits that are not valued, in fact are often a liability, in the business world.

Then came the feminist revolution, and suddenly all the rules changed. Women finally got in the "game" so to speak. They began pursuing and taking the opportunities they considered to be rightfully theirs, no longer willing to sit on the sidelines while the men had all the fun. Over the last two decades, women have demonstrated that they can be every bit as capable as their male counterparts in every area of life — business, sports, medicine, law, education, you name it.

But we are still learning the rules — especially those that define how to compete effectively and successfully — because as young girls we were never given the chance to develop that skill. So we must do it now.

With this book I hope to take the first step toward achieving that goal. The information I share in the following chapters comes from observation, personal experience, and interviews with women leaders in both the public and private sector. By heightening awareness of the negative, competitive behavior that is dragging us down, I hope to show that the problem is real — but that the solution is in our hands.

As women of high standards and healthy ambition, let's take this next important step in our development as the female leaders of the twenty-first century, ready to compete at every level with integrity and intelligence and the skills to survive.

Survival of the Fittest

Like it or not, our society — and especially our economy — is driven by competition. The freedom to compete we as Americans enjoy is one of the primary reasons the U.S. has attained its stature as the most influential country in the world. Competition allows the status quo to be challenged; it encourages us to develop our resources and improve ourselves.

Our economy also functions on a model of scarcity; in the business world that means that there are usually several people competing for each desirable position for which there can only be one person chosen. This point is especially important for woman professionals, because traditionally opportunities for them to succeed have been so few, and that makes the competition all the more fierce.

It's easy to see how some women can feel driven to use whatever means available to ensure that they are the ones chosen. This pressure to succeed, coupled with the fear that if they don't get the job, the promotion or raise, they might never get another opportunity. This dilemma can push women into taking desperate actions.

Before we can decide on what we can do to change how we compete with each other, let's examine the way we go about it now, using my own experiences as an example.

When I entered the business world, I was enthusiastic and full of optimism and ambition. I had every reason to feel that way: Not only had I risen to the top of the corporate structure in record time, I had done so with the help of powerful women executives. Don't get me wrong; I had worked hard to get where I was. But I planned to work even harder to justify the faith others had put in me, to contribute to the common good with the newfound power I had been given.

Like most women who have risen to the top, I began in an entry-level position. I set my sights high, seeing myself as someone who was pursuing the American dream. My co-workers saw me as arrogant and ambitious. "Just who does she think she is?" they sniped. Employees at the next level, the middle managers, distrusted me as someone who couldn't be counted on to stay in her place. These attitudes confused me; I thought we were all trying to work hard and get ahead. Because I was succeeding, those who were not resented me.

With determination and luck, I climbed the career ladder quickly, finding myself in upper management in less than two years. In my new executive position, I was certain that the mean-spirited pettiness I had encountered during my climb would be left behind. Finally, I thought to myself, I would be working with professionals who didn't need to undermine their associates to get ahead. I would soon learn otherwise.

Alley Cats

When I reached the hallowed halls of the executive elite, I was intimidated by the power surrounding me. I admit that at first I was afraid to walk the "alleys," as those halls were known. But I learned to be what I now call an "alley cat," someone wise in the ways of playing the game like the others did in the alley — not fair, out-in-the-open competition, but getting the job done by any means possible.

Because my nature is to be straightforward, honest, even outspoken at times, I found it difficult to play these games. I wondered why we women were competing on such a personal and emotional level, feeling that the only way to help ourselves was to hurt each other. After months of observation, I believe I figured it out.

To compete means to differentiate oneself from others. As women, this goes against our very nature, for we have evolved to be cooperative creatures. But if we are to compete, and win, we feel we must stand apart from other women. Because differentiating ourselves doesn't feel natural, however, it frightens us, making us feel that we are on our own and will end up alone and abandoned.

And, so, when we see another woman who isn't afraid to compete, who effectively stands apart from the rest of us, we feel envy. We perceive her as more accomplished, more successful than we are, able to do what we cannot do.

Envy can be understood as a form of thwarted identification, a desire for sameness, not difference. Unlike jealousy, which indicates a perceived loss, envy implies desire, in this case the desire for a connection, which we feel is disrupted by the necessity to be different if we want to compete.

Envy — and how we as women express our envy — is the enemy. I've witnessed behavior so cruel and demeaning that I thought I was watching some overwrought Hollywood soap opera. I have been shocked and appalled at the devious planning and plotting that went on, not because the victim of these conniving machinations deserved it, but because her coworkers' envy over her possible success made them take extraordinary steps. These women let their envy override their good sense, feeling that if they couldn't move up, they would drag their competitor down any way they could.

This is no way for us to lead our daughters, nor our sons for that matter. If we want to truly achieve success, to rise to a level of power that we deserve and can maintain, to be great leaders, we must return to our true nature — that of nurturing, mentoring, collaborating. Instead of crucifying each other in the boardroom, which will eventually come back to haunt us, we need to seek the high road, work to lift the spirits of ourselves and others. If we do not learn to compete this way, we will squander the hard-won advances we have made in the last two decades.

And, so, with this book, I hope to encourage all women in the workplace to develop strategies for competing that serve our needs and further our development as professionals and leaders.

Reach high, for stars lie hidden in your soul.
Dream deep, for every dream precedes the goal.
—Pamela Vaull Starr

That Competitive Edge

I have come to think of my career as a race I am running in which I am one of many competitors. My goal is to run the best race I can, to sail over each hurdle, to reach the finish line first — in essence, to do better than my opponents. This doesn't mean that I resort to any means possible to beat them; I've got to run a clean race, drawing on my own resources, hard work, and skills to do the best I can. I hope I win, but if I don't, I can still congratulate the winner and know that there will be other races to run.

With this archetype in mind, I've broken down this "race" into various "legs" and will share with you what I think is the important focus of each phase, what you want to be doing at every step along the way so that you compete at your best.

FIRST LEG

The Starting Line

On your mark, get set, go!

Beginning the race is often the most difficult part, for, in the words of one astute observer, if you don't know where you want to go, you will certainly never get there. Have that finish line in sight by identifying your goals — you'll have a clearer vision as to what you need to do to reach them.

When I first entered the workforce, I was a lowly clerk within a government agency. It didn't take me long to realize that the job I held would not satisfy me; I coveted the prized management positions of those employees several rungs up the ladder and felt that, given the opportunity, I could do a good job at that level. Although I didn't have a clue as to how to get to that elevated position, I didn't let that deter me. I set my goal and then went after it. What did I have to lose? I began to plot my strategy.

My first step was to examine the hierarchy of agencies and their employees throughout the state. Through research, I identified which agency would offer me the best opportunity for upward mobility. I had officially completed Step I: I had begun the race and I knew where the finish line was.

When you decide you want to position yourself for a leadership position, strategy is key. The following exercise will give you some specific ideas on how you can begin your own race. Keep a journal to answer these questions for easy reference.

What type of a career am I looking for? What level do I seek: supervisory, middle management, or executive management? How do I get there? How soon can I get there?

- ◆ Set time frames

- ◆ Seek guidance from a career counselor

- ◆ Self-develop (attend seminars and conferences, get a coach, or go back to school)

- ◆ Identify any qualifications for jobs you want to pursue

- ◆ Do you have the necessary skills? If not, how do you obtain them?

- ◆ Prepare yourself. It is better to be prepared for an opportunity that does not present itself, than to have an opportunity present itself and not be prepared.

SECOND LEG

Building Up Steam

You're off and running; now your goal is to establish a pace. By this I mean that, in whatever position you have taken, you must make sure that you consistently deliver what you have agreed to do. If you promise more than you can produce, you will lose credibility and slide backward in the race. It's far better to start small, do a good job and finish a task on time, thereby demonstrating that you can be counted on to accomplish what you commit to.

Once you've established that you are competent and trustworthy, and if you're ready to work even harder to get to the next level, then move on to the next step by requesting additional work. By doing so, you will prove your initiative and become an invaluable member of the team. And, when the boss is looking for someone whom he or she can count on, your name will be first on the list.

Yes, what I'm suggesting is difficult — plain, old-fashioned, nose-to-the-grindstone labor. But it works. I know, because I used this strategy myself, taking home work at night and on weekends so that I could complete not only my assigned duties, but additional projects as well. My initiative earned me the recognition that eventually helped me move up several rungs on that ladder.

The most common attribute identified in women who achieve high-level success in corporate America is the ability to produce.

The following are some of the strategies common to women who succeed which you, too, can use:

- ◆ Strive to consistently exceed performance expectations

- ◆ Develop a style that men are comfortable with

- ◆ Seek difficult or high-visibility assignments

- ◆ Recruit an influential mentor

- ◆ Network with influential colleagues

- ◆ Gain line-management experience

- ◆ Move from one functional area to another

- ◆ Initiate discussion regarding career aspirations

- ◆ Be able to relocate

- ◆ Upgrade educational credentials

- ◆ Change companies or agencies if necessary

- ◆ Develop leadership opportunities outside the office

- ◆ Gain national and international experience

Besides superior performance, the only other strategy regarded as critical to a woman's advancement is developing a style with which male managers are comfortable. These included such traits as having a sense of humor, maintaining an energetic and positive attitude, being a team player, possessing good people-management skills, and being adept at problem solving. These skills are not gender-based, however, they are essential to the success of both men and women.

THIRD LEG

Sailing Over the Hurdles

This is the part of the race that's the most challenging and the most fun. You've hit your stride, you're feeling good — and now you're going to be tested.

In my case, I had proven myself at a lower level, and now I was ready to move on up. Again, I found that I had to be the one to make that happen, so I devised what I thought was a bold plan.

Elections had been recently held in our state and a new governor had been installed. Knowing that people and positions were probably in a state of flux, I set out to meet the new governor, hoping to find a spot in that administration.

First I went shopping at a store that catered to business-women on a limited budget where I bought three business suits with interchangeable jackets. Next, I checked the newspaper daily to find out which public receptions would be given in the governor's honor. Then, with business cards at the ready in my suit pocket, I attended every reception I could and made sure I got in the receiving line. Each time I shook the governor's hand, I handed him a card on which I had written on the back: "I have been recognized as a candidate for a management position within my agency."

After the sixth or seventh reception, the governor began to recognize me. He must have liked my determination because he called the director of my agency and said, "I keep running into this woman who's looking for a job in your cabinet. Would you take a look at her?" The director agreed and I had my foot in the door.

The director gave me two assignments. The first sent me to St. Petersburg, Russia, where I helped train Russian officials on how to mediate legal cases. In the second, I served as the lead person in the reorganization of the second largest program within a 2500-employee organization. (Two unbelievable chances to prove myself, right? But I was ready for them because I had taken on that additional work and pursued those educational opportunities others had turned down.) I performed well in both and was eventually recommended for promotion into executive management.

There are lots of ways you can get your name and face in front of the right people. Be creative. Be proactive. The following are a few ideas to get you started.

Volunteer

Here's something everybody can do. There are any number of organizations that need help — public and private. You can pick one that will give you some experience and visibility in the career you've decided to pursue. Don't worry that you may not have any skills they can use. Start out as an envelope stuffer and work your way up.

Serve on Boards or Commissions

This may sound difficult, but it's easily attainable if you are willing to put in some time and effort. For example, if you enjoy the public library, start attending meetings of the board. Be visible, ask questions, introduce yourself. Get on the Internet and educate yourself on the issues facing libraries today. When it comes time to appoint a new board member, people will remember your genuine interest. This is called positioning and it works.

Attend Political Receptions

This is my old trick and, as you can see, it worked for me. It's just another form of networking, one in which you must take the initiative. But that persistence will be a positive trait that people will remember. Make sure you are courteous and well-groomed, because you are counting on people remembering you by the impression you made.

Work On Campaigns

This can be exhaustive, but it's a great way to connect with people who are the movers and the shakers. You'll acquire a lot of political savvy, see how things really get done, learn how to negotiate, and probably have some fun.

Start a Card File on People You Know

Now that you've had all these exciting experiences, start a file on all of the people you've met. List their name, affiliation (how you know them), and anything about them that might help you in the future. Again, this is another networking tool, a way of broadening your horizons with the people and experiences of your life.

Meet Influential People

All the while you are attending political receptions, working on campaigns, doing volunteer work, sitting in on council meetings, or whatever strategy you decide to follow, make a point to get to know people, introduce yourself and make an appointment with them to discuss issues. Other people do it, and so can you.

FOURTH LEG

Hitting the Wall

I had reached the top, or so I thought, and I assumed I would be able to do my job without interference from other employees who resented or were threatened by me. Instead I hit the wall — the most painful and trying part of any race, as runners will tell you. In my case, the wall I encountered was erected by my female counterparts who felt my quick rise to prominence was unfair to those who had taken much longer to get where I was.

I was hurt and disheartened by the isolation, ridicule, and, in some cases, outright sabotage that confronted me. There were times when I wondered whether reaching my goal was worth going through all this anguish.

But, just like runners who experience this phenomenon, I knew that if I wanted to keep going, I had to develop the powers of endurance. I found the following Chinese maxim, which inspired me to push through the pain:

Endure by Enduring
Understanding the difficulties,
Enduring the hardships,
Predicting the risks,
Tolerating the abuse;
For such a person,
All ensure fame and success.

If you find yourself in this same place — and if you're going to be out in the competitive workplace, you will no doubt encounter it at some point — here are some things you can do. Let's look at this poem and see how its points can be put into practice.

Understand the Difficulties

Learn how to walk that fine line between cynicism and naiveté. Understand that opposition can arise where you least expect it. Expect the best, but prepare for the worst.

Endure the Hardships

If you are to weather the difficult times, you will need a strategy. Mine was to find a confidant, someone whom I could trust to be objective and truthful. Because my problems came from other women, I asked a man, a fellow executive team member, to act as my confidant. He helped me keep things in perspective and gave me constructive criticism that I knew was not politically motivated. He played a vital role in keeping me focused on success rather than failure.

Predicting the Risk

When you understand the attitudes of the people with whom you are working as well as the environment of your particular workplace, you give yourself a tremendous advantage. If you are about to make a risky decision, do your homework. Find and recruit your allies so that you increase the strength of your position. Not only will it be easier to make

your decision stick, you'll have a better idea ahead of time if
what you plan is ill-advised.

Tolerating the Abuse

This is perhaps the most difficult challenge. The abuse
may be overt or covert, but you will most certainly encounter it somewhere along the way. Think of it as an opportunity
to show what you're really made of. Keep your dignity and
self-respect by refusing to stoop to your abuser's level. If you
must retaliate, do so openly and honestly, with logic rather
than emotion. You will maintain your integrity and earn the
respect of others.

I framed the endurance poem and hung it on the wall
in my office for a quick reference when the going got tough.
It helped me keep my sanity and on more than one occa-
sion.

The Finish Line

If you follow these four steps, I am confident that you
will reach your goal. But, beware, for even though you have
entered the winner's circle, your most difficult challenge
may still lie ahead. You will have won the short race; now
you must prepare for the long-distance run, one that may
seem more like an obstacle course as you make your way
through it.

Let's look at some of the pitfalls you will want to avoid as you continue to compete at your highest level:

1.   Yackity-Yak! Don't Talk Back! (Gossip)

Gossip, gossip, gossip. It's an inevitable, irresistible pastime found in every office. It may seem harmless, but it can bring you down. What's more, savvy and unscrupulous people know how to use gossip to further their own agendas — usually at someone else's expense.

Because of our collaborative, social nature, we like to engage in social conversation. At one point in my career I made the mistake of engaging in what I thought was a friendly conversation with my peers. I was trying to connect with them, to be one of the girls, to earn their trust. In retrospect I can see that I shared too much about myself, and I unwittingly played into the hands of my rivals. Some innocent remarks I had made were embellished and turned against me; allegations were made and I had to spend a lot of time and effort clearing my name.

I had been so busy trying to be everyone's friend that I didn't realize I had put myself in a vulnerable position. I hadn't done anything different than any of my coworkers — but a couple of them were looking for a way to sabotage my success, and I handed it to them on a silver platter.

I learned from my mistake, and you can, too. Don't get involved in office gossip. Be wary of others who want to draw you into their confidence, to share their secrets with you. Make it clear that you're too busy to listen; or, if you can't escape, don't contribute in any way. You will quickly communicate that you are not going to play the game, and you will maintain your integrity and earn the respect of others.

2. I Hope She Dies... (Envy)

As I explained before, envy is an insidious emotion, one to which we women are particularly susceptible because of the evolutionary traits of our gender. But we don't have to succumb to it. As soon as you feel its icy grip, stop it in its tracks. Ask yourself why you are feeling this way. Take an honest look at yourself and your situation; identify what the problem is and what you can do about it.

I once was hired into an executive position alongside another woman who was better educated, more experienced, and more capable than I — and who never let me forget it. I came to resent her need to make me feel inferior, but I still envied what she represented.

Finally I realized that stewing in my own juices wasn't getting me anywhere. I stopped to analyze the situation rationally rather than emotionally. Okay, I said to myself, she is more accomplished than I am. What am I going to do about it?

Just stepping back and honestly evaluating the problem started me down the right road. I decided to take steps to change my situation. I began by attending every relevant seminar and training event I could. Encouraged by my success, I went back to school full-time in the evenings, finally getting my bachelor's degree in business. Next I attended the Strategic Leadership Program at Duke University, followed by the Executive Leadership Program at the University of Washington. Finally, I was selected by the governor to attend the Executive State and Local Government Program at the John F. Kennedy School of Government at Harvard University.

Obviously, my transformation did not happen overnight. However, I no longer envy her — or anyone, for that matter, because I learned that that kind of thinking will get me nowhere.

The point is, don't waste time wallowing in envy; it won't improve the situation, but it will certainly diminish you. Instead, use that emotional energy to propel yourself forward to beat your rivals at their own game.

A favorite book of mine, *Thick Face, Black Heart,* by author Chin-Ning Chu, has a saying to which I often refer: "The opportunity for victory is sometimes provided by the enemy."

When you find yourself feeling envy over what someone else has, look on it as a motivator to move you forward
in your pursuits.

3.   How Did She Get That Job? (Jealousy)

Jealousy is similar to envy, in that we are overcome by
this destructive emotion when we feel a perceived loss. It is
a demeaning, debilitating, paralyzing trait, and can bring
down even the biggest of the big-wigs.

Jealousy can rear its ugly head where you least expect
it. For example, you may find that the very person whom you
respect and rely upon, and who helped you reach your goal,
may turn around and be jealous of the qualities you possess
that brought you to your success. It's a sorry fact that some
women, fueled by jealousy and consumed by the pursuit of
their own goals, will act the role of supporter to a coworker
— only to use this position of intimacy to undermine the very
person who trusts them.

Jealousy can also seriously threaten the effectiveness of
a team. One East Coast interviewee recalled her experiences
in an office where a team of women executives constantly
competed for funding for their projects. But, because they
were motivated by jealousy — especially if one team member was perceived as receiving more than her share — their
competing took on the form of character assassination, behind-the-scenes plotting, and outright deception. In this case,

competition fueled by jealousy completely demoralized the team.

You must be vigilant about jealousy, as it can defeat you in two ways. First, and perhaps the most destructive to you, is when you succumb to jealous feelings. If you do find your-self feeling jealous, don't beat yourself up; jealousy, after all, is a very human reaction. Instead, resolve to recognize it when it appears, and then redirect your efforts so that you do not fall into its trap.

Second, be aware that others feel jealousy too; with every success you attain, you can be sure that there is some-one hoping to snatch it away from you. This aspect is the more difficult to deal with, for you may not realize just who is jealous of you and secretly working against you. You must simply focus on doing your job; enlist support but be be-holden to no one. Choose your allies well, and emphasize a collaborative rather than combative work environment.

4. "Of Course, I Had Nothing To Do With That." (Lying)

In my opinion, lying is the most despicable — and un-forgivable — behavior I have witnessed in a professional setting.

I understand that the truth is rarely absolute; it comes in varying shades, colored by recollection or point of view. For example, Freud put forth the theory of "willing back-ward," the process of rearranging accounts of past events in order to endow them with a different meaning. And most of us have revised our own history somewhat, justifying our selective memory as a way to better influence our patterns for the future. Let's face it, who hasn't put some "spin" on a story to make it all the more entertaining in the telling?

When I speak of lying, I am not referring to these examples; no, I mean those instances in which a person deliberately and knowingly misrepresents the facts for their own personal gain.

Lying never works. There is always some point at which the liar will be caught, and what ensues is often more destructive than the original lie.

Take the example one woman executive in New York discussed in her interview. She was a member of a team whose leader had revealed some developments on a sensitive issue, asking that they keep the information confidential so as not to interfere with the necessary processes for resolution of the problem. All gave their word — but one did not keep it, instead meddling to influence the outcome.

When confronted by the team leader with her actions, this woman lied about her tampering, using tears and recriminations to make her story more credible. The leader backed down, revoking his reprimand. And what did the woman do? She boasted to the others about her ability to lie and get away with it.

Unfortunately, although her little ruse worked and she got off the hook, she destroyed the integrity of the team forever. Seeing that lying brought no dire consequences — not to mention that she wasn't reprimanded for the original infraction — other team members considered using the same tactics. Trust diminished, confrontations increased, the desire to work together evaporated. The group became dysfunctional and had to be disbanded.

And what happened to the woman? Because lying had worked for her, she continued to lie when she needed to squeeze out of a tight spot. But, as is inevitable with liars, she eventually got caught, and all of the deceit she had practiced over the years was uncovered. Her career and her reputation were ruined forever. And although she made the choice herself, still it was sad to see the grim consequences of her actions.

5.   The Alley Cat Syndrome (Corruption)

This is one of the most disappointing and demoralizing aspects of success we must change. Women finally make it to the "executive alley" only to find that it is a dark and treacherous place — not at all what they expected.

That's how it happened for me. My rise had been rapid and, I'll admit it, I was naive; I hadn't had time to realize how the political games were played. I was thrilled to be in the rarefied air of upper management. I figured I had already overcome the most difficult hurdles. I'd made it into the big time, and from now on I could play the game to create positive change. Unfortunately, the other women were playing for personal gain. They saw me as an upstart, a threat, someone who could put them on the sidelines. I soon learned they would do whatever it took to defend their territory.

For the first few weeks I didn't know what hit me. I felt like I was wearing a bulls-eye on my back, as I became a target for the deceit, manipulation, and downright dishonesty of others. But, I soon adapted, learning to play the game just like the big girls, and I began to resort to the same type of tactics.

What I didn't know then was that competing in this negative way was hurting me on a number of levels. First, it was diverting time and energy from my duties as an executive. I'd worked hard to get to the top and yet I was jeopardizing my position by giving too much of my attention to office politics. Second, it was turning me into the kind of person I despised. I had bought into the philosophy that the best defense is a good offense, and I began engaging in that behind-the-scenes kind of plotting that I hated.

Negative competition reflects a low self-esteem, an insecurity that translates strengths into weaknesses, self-assertion into self-denial. When we resort to underhanded tactics, we are saying that we have no faith in our own ability to pursue our goals openly. We trust neither ourselves nor our counterparts and feel our only path to power is through indirect tactics and sometimes mercenary means.

I believe that if we as women are ever going to be truly in the game — not just second-string players but the stars, the ones who shape the future — then we have to break this pattern of corruption of our values. And we can do that by learning not only how to compete, but how to lead with a wise and generous spirit.

Losing the Race

I can't leave this topic without saying a few words about failure.

Let's face it, you're probably going to lose more races than you win, but that's okay. Even if you don't always succeed at what you try, you are still taking the initiative, assuming a risk, going after what you want. The more attempts you make, the better your chances are of eventually reaching your goals. You can't let failing deter you; in fact, failure is one of the most valuable teaching tools you will ever find. It provides you with the impetus and information to move in new directions.

The good news is that, as a society, we tend to forget failure and remember success. That is how it should be, for it often takes countless attempts before we accomplish what we set out to do. And when we fail, we are in good company. How many times did Edison unsuccessfully try to light up the incandescent light bulb? How many times did the Wright brothers fall to earth in their flying machines? Nobody cares! All we remember, and celebrate, is that they kept trying and finally succeeded, making incredible contributions that improved our lives forever.

In the most basic sense, our response to failure can be seen as evolutionary adaptation; in other words, those of us who do not learn to adapt become extinct. The roads of evolution are strewn with the bones of creatures who did not adjust to their changing environment. In the business world, to refuse to adapt translates into being passed over for promotion, losing an account, not getting a job, or just becoming irrelevant. To survive, or in our case, to succeed, we must learn from our failures and be willing to make whatever changes are necessary.

As I mentioned before, when I was catapulted into the executive alley, I found myself suddenly thrust into a negatively competitive environment. Hurt and resentful, I let my wounded ego determine my actions. I became distant and nonparticipatory. I stopped speaking to certain people, wouldn't work on teams with anyone I didn't like, refused to talk in meetings for fear of giving others ammunition against me. Although I was publicly silent, behind the scenes I had become a street-wise alley cat, skilled at playing vengeful and vindictive games, stooping to the lowest level to further my agenda. I had lost the battle, but I had not lost the war!

One day it hit home that I had become someone I didn't respect. Even though my tactics had brought me some power, I took no pride in my position. I knew this was not the way to compete, much less lead, and I did not want this kind of duplicitous behavior to be my legacy. I felt I didn't deserve to rise to the top if I refused to handle my problems in the open. Instead of shutting out my adversaries, I had to learn how to meet them on common ground.

If I had kept on using the same tactics, there is no doubt in my mind that I would have been left behind. Instead, I decided to make some changes. I analyzed my deficiencies and sought new skills to improve myself. I learned how to adapt to the various situations I encountered, and I did that by understanding how to align reality with values.

When I returned to Harvard to pursue my Master's degree, I had the privilege of studying the art of value-laden leadership under a profound professor who is a recognized authority on the subject. I learned where I had failed in the past and developed new techniques and strategies for future leadership positions.

For example, in my first leadership position after graduation, I was given an assignment to work on a project to reorganize a human resource office for a large corporation. I immediately ran into a confrontation with my assigned partner over an issue regarding reporting structures. If I were still operating in my old way, I would have backed away publicly from my position, but worked covertly to make sure I got my way. This kind of short-term thinking is selfish and nonproductive.

Instead, I asked myself the following questions:

◆ What are we missing here?

◆ Are we suppressing the values of competing groups rather than trying to understand the true problem at hand?

◆ Are there shared values that might enable us to engage in a dialogue about our competing views and find a compatible solution?

In this case, I realized that my values as an African-American woman and my partner's values as a Caucasian male were in opposition and therefore interfering with resolving the problem at hand.

Once we addressed these differences in values, we were able to find common ground, and we eventually devised a compromise that we could both live with.

*Child, don't come with any bent over shoulders, stand up;
let the world see you coming.*
— Shirley Chisholm, first African American women
elected to the U.S. Congress

The Big Race

I have focused so far on competition and the ways in which women have traditionally competed and how they must develop more constructive methods for competing in the future. One reason for this change of style is obvious: When we learn new techniques for competing and interacting with one another in ways that promote rather than destroy our female counterparts, we will inevitably succeed. But there is a larger, more important reason to learn how to compete with integrity — and that is so we can become better leaders.

America is in dire need of leaders in general — and women leaders in particular. Again, just as it is true with competition, women in our country have not had many opportunities to lead, and so we must acquire these skills if we are to continue forward in our progress. Before I talk about how women can continue to lead, however, let's examine the framework of leadership as espoused by Dr. Ronald Heifetz in his book *Leadership Without Easy Answers.*

Traditionally, scholars have defined leadership as value-free, because this definition lends itself more easily to analytical study, in essence placing it in a vacuum for them to poke and probe. But in the real world, does this value-free definition of leadership work? The intent of this book, is to encourage you to define leadership as an activity based upon values.

Leaders arouse passion because they engage our values. We respect leaders like Mandela for their courage and commitment, we respond to their character and charisma, and we expect them to reflect the values we honor. Even those leaders who are morally corrupt still have the power to coalesce a strong feeling of loyalty among their followers, because their leadership mirrors that group's values. Leaders of inner-city gangs, or the messianic leaders of cults such as Waco or Jonestown, are good examples.

And we, as followers, have added other values to the concept of leadership as well; because leaders typically hold high office or exert great influence, we accord them power and station. We are communicating that the power that comes with leadership has its own intrinsic worth.

Throughout history, leadership has meant possessing the power to influence a group of people to follow the leader's vision. Because the leader reflects the group's values, the group transfers their power to that leader. The key factor of this traditional paradigm of leadership is influence.

The community of followers looks to the leader for deliverance from their problem and then abdicates involvement or responsibility. If something goes wrong, the fault lies with the leader; the followers, who have been nothing more than sheep, are left without any direction nor any hope of knowing how to direct themselves, so they blame the leader for any failure.

Dr. Heifetz, however, proposes a different approach to leadership, one where the leader inspires the community to face its problem and actively engage in finding the solution. Influence still plays a role, but the measure of leadership here is the progress the group and the leader make together toward solving the problem. The leader is not trying to lead the group in following her vision; instead, she is challenging them to collaborate on finding their own vision and, ultimately, take ownership of the solution.

Mobilizing — the act of motivating, organizing, orienting, and focusing attention — people to tackle tough problems is the definition Dr. Heifetz applies to the concept of leadership. I've had the opportunity to apply his theory in a business setting and I know just how well this principle works in actual practice. I recommend using this definition as a yardstick to measure leaders from all walks of life — even, and perhaps especially, to measure yourself.

Remember our earlier discussion about learning to adapt? Adaptive work is especially important in the art of leadership. Whereas the old, outdated style of leadership might rely on persuasion, coercion, or even denial to temporarily overcome differing factions in a community, the new standard of leadership calls for recognition of conflicts in the group and necessitates working together to diminish the gap between the values people hold and the reality they face.

It is clear, then, that the leaders who will successfully take us into the next millennium are those who are adept at showing followers how to adapt — meaning how to make necessary changes in their values, beliefs, or behavior. Their ability to expose conflict and orchestrate resolution within constituencies will give them the leverage to mobilize people to learn new ways.

The fact that the parameters for what it takes to lead are changing provides an advantage to women. Not only does this mean that men have to learn all over again how to lead — thus leveling the playing field for the sexes — but this new style of leadership is actually more in keeping with the collaborative nature of women.

But as women we have our own work to do if we are to move into the leadership positions of the future. We are still confronted by a scarcity of positions at the top, and this fuels our fear that we won't be one of the chosen few. So, while many women may say they want to see a diversified female executive administration, what they really mean is that they want the workforce diversified as long as the jobs at the top stay within their grasp.

If we are ever to break through the barriers that confine women in our pursuit of success, we will only be able to do so by inclusion rather than exclusion. We cannot simply accept that there are very few spots available and beat each other to a pulp trying to be one of the few to secure one. We must work together to make sure that more top-level positions are available to women. And the only way to do that is by helping each of us develop into better candidates — women supporting women in becoming more educated, more experienced, more savvy, more skilled — so that there is such a large pool of qualified women that we will naturally be considered and chosen for upper management positions, just as men are today.

For women, acknowledging our competition with each other is living dangerously. Being responsible for it is courageous. Changing our society, changing ourselves is significant.

—Laura Tracey, author

The Challenge of Champions

As women we have a number of challenges awaiting us. First and foremost is learning how to compete. Second is embracing the idea of supporting each other and mentoring those who come behind us. And third is acquiring the skills and the determination to lead both women and men into new areas of achievement.

Women are poised to be at the forefront of leadership in the twenty-first century because we find ourselves in the embryonic stage of our evolution as competitors and leaders. Since we are at the beginning of the learning curve, we do not have to undo years of conditioning, of "we've always done it that way" kind of thinking.

Of course, up to this point we have most often been led by men who practice traditional leadership. From those experiences, I deduced that leadership meant shaping a vision, providing direction, exerting influence, solving problems, and protecting one's followers. And while these traits are still somewhat evident in the new, emerging philosophy of leadership, the focus is quite different.

Now I identify leadership in terms of the ability to employ the principles of adaptive work — which means recognizing and addressing conflicts in the values the followers hold, and then working to diminish the gap between those values and the reality they face. Leadership still confers a measure of authority on the leader, but she must be able to apply that authority through adaptive work.

A true leader, then, knows how to use power, influence, and authority as tools to mobilize others into adaptive work. Instead of coercing followers into a single vision, a leader enlists their participation in the process by asking such questions as: How do we get to the purpose of the organization? How do we do the work? How do we measure progress? How do we manage conflict and adaptations?

As we evolve into this new and more complex definition of leadership, we still need to remember essential elements to help us succeed. Leaders must:

- ♦ Understand and communicate the purpose of the organization

- ♦ Maintain a clear focus

- ♦ Establish clear rules and expectations

- ♦ Stay alert to the changing environment

- Identify threats

- Build relationships and gain allies (leadership does not mean "stand alone")

- Give members what they need to do their work (space, supplies, support, clear specifications, avenues of recourse)

- Expect adaptive work which meets the set standards (good quality, timely, effective, efficient)

With these guidelines in place, a team can create relationships of trust, gain respect for each other, feel secure in their role within the team, and become allies. The leader is then free to problem solve, identify and correct inappropriate dependencies, such as the habit of some members to seek solutions from authority, and maintain a holding environment.

When a diverse group of people come together to work as a team in a professional setting, conflict will inevitably arise. The negative emotions that erupt can stifle the creativity of the group and often intimidate into silence those who have something valuable to contribute. During these times of instability, the leader can use the holding environment strategy to restore order and mutual respect.

The term "holding environment" originated in psychoanalysis to describe the relationship between the therapist and the patient. The therapist "holds" the patient in a process of developmental learning in a way that is similar to how a parent surrounds a child within a blanket of security, allowing the child to explore her world without feeling vulnerable. The therapist functions in much the same manner, offering a safe haven, a protected place where the patient can examine his fears, problems, crises, and choices, and contemplate what direction to move in before making a commitment to taking any action.

A leader can provide similar support to those team members who are afraid to move forward within the group. By empathizing with the person and demonstrating an understanding of the nature of the problem, the leader creates the necessary holding environment. The distressed team member is given the opportunity to stop, analyze, and decide how to progress, without fear of interference or repercussions from other members of the group.

This technique requires both skill and expertise, and many people in leadership positions are neither qualified nor interested in employing such an approach. I witnessed one such example when I worked on a team where one of the members, a woman, consistently held differing opinions on issues we faced. Because of her point of view, she and her ideas were largely ignored; understandably, she became silent, unproductive, and nonparticipatory, and eventually left the team. Had the holding environment procedure been conducive to the needs of all the team members, her perspective would have been accorded the same significance as that of the rest of the group, and the team as a whole would have benefited from her unique position.

Live as if you were to die tomorrow. Learn as if you were to live forever.

—Gandhi

The Leader as Coach

As mentioned before, the concept of leadership is shifting — from authoritative to adaptive, from all-knowing savior to consensus-building coach. The leader's role now is not so much to tell the team members what to do, but to provide the means for each member to perform at his or her best.

To do this takes an investment of time and the application of tools that will illuminate the values of each of the team's members. There are a number of ways in which to elicit this information; one of the most effective is profiling, where each person in the group — including the leader — answers a series of questions designed to disclose the different qualities and values within each person. The Meyer-Briggs test is one of the most popular of these kinds of questionnaires.

The results of these tests are made public to the entire group; many leaders will instigate discussion on what was found. This openness establishes an atmosphere of trust, and as the profiles are examined, the group as a whole becomes more aware of the dynamics within the team. With this knowledge in hand, members are more likely to feel secure in making creative suggestions — and be more tolerant of differing opinions.

As she coaches each member of her team, a leader must remember to distinguish her role from her self. This is often one of the biggest challenges in providing leadership, for as the leader makes unpopular decisions, some members will no doubt react negatively. When faced with animosity, dissension, and resentment, it is only human nature to respond in kind. But the leader cannot afford this luxury; instead, she must recognize these emotions as reactions to the role she plays and the perspective she represents, rather than a criticism of her intrinsic self.

Distinguishing role from self enables the leader to avoid being misled by her emotions into taking statements and events personally. When tough situations arise, she makes the distinction and externalizes the conflict, thereby focusing attention on the issues and giving the conflict back to its rightful owner. The leader then guides the team to work through the problem using adaptive techniques.

The leader must be the one who takes into account the big picture, who refuses to be sidetracked by personal issues and petty politics. Think again of the coach, climbing up into the stands to take a good look at the team. From that vantage point, she can gain a detached, impartial, comprehensive overview and see what works and what doesn't.

Let's examine a leadership strategy as applied to competing interests within a team.

A CEO of a major corporation, looking to create a more balanced executive management team, wants to develop a plan for recruiting and retaining more women. This CEO calls a meeting of the executive team members, puts forth the initiative, and asks for feedback. When everyone agrees and offers a multitude of resources to accomplish the goal, the leader is surprised, having expected a spectrum of responses due to the make-up of the group. Their unqualified enthusiasm raises questions about whether each member feels confident in putting forth his or her true opinion. Hidden agendas may also be lurking beneath their ready acquiescence.

To clarify the team's true character and direction, the CEO devises a multipronged strategy. If she has not done so already, the leader first conducts a reality test, using one of the many methods available to define each member's personal attributes and qualities. With the results of this test in hand, the team as a whole now understands more fully each member's technical competence, managerial experience, behavioral patterns, and personal needs. The leader also gains insight on how to influence different team members to work within the team more effectively.

Next, the leader mobilizes the team members to progress toward the goal through adaptive work, which includes shifting values, beliefs, or behaviors. In this step, the leader is not only providing a guide for goal formation, but using that goal as a means to motivate the team to face rather than avoid tough realities and conflicts.

The most difficult yet most valuable task of leadership may be advancing goals and designing strategies that promote adaptive work. The third component of this leader's plan is to work with the team to come up with the specific procedure that will get them to their goal.

It is at this point in the process that conflict, if it has not already appeared, is most likely to break out and the real work begins. The leader must return to what she knows about each of the team members and ask some defining questions:

- What is causing the distress?

- What internal contradictions does the distress represent?

- What are the histories of these contradictions?

- What perspectives and interests have various team members come to represent to various segments of the community that are now in conflict?

- In what way are we in the organization or group mirroring the problem dynamics in the community?

When the CEO first introduced her suggestion, team members were not willing to face stress, and by their agreement they kept what is known as a state of equilibrium or balance within the team. But as the leader moved the team toward the goal, differences emerged and the team became unbalanced, in distress, operating from chaos. There are any number of ways to get the team back into balance; many of them are merely evasive tactics, known as work avoidance mechanisms such as blaming authority, scapegoating, externalizing the enemy, denying the problem, or finding a distracting issue.

It is the leader who must bring the members back to the table to engage in the adaptive work that will truly restore their equilibrium. Holding on to past assumptions, blind spots, hidden agendas, and other defeative behavior must be, and can be, exposed with the help of the reality testing done in the first stage of the leader's strategy. Even though taking these actions will generate stress and resistance, it will ultimately teach the team members how to adapt, so that they can reach a goal that otherwise would be unattainable.

Character cannot be developed in ease and quiet. Only through experiences of trial and suffering can the soul be strengthened, vision cleared, ambition inspired and success achieved. Face your deficiencies and acknowledge them, but do not let them master you.

—Helen Keller

Successes

Each step on the path to a higher standard of leadership takes courage. When you find the courage to commit to absolute values and to the universal code of conduct to treat others as you would like to be treated yourself, you will succeed as a leader.

Leaders who consistently and successfully lead their followers are those who:

◆ Accord mutual respect

◆ Listen to others

◆ Remain open to new ideas

◆ Create a supportive environment that nurtures personal and professional growth

◆ Nourish their soul and their spirit

◆ Refuse to be silenced

◆ Distinguish themselves from their role

- ◆ Externalize conflict

- ◆ Control their own hunger (their needs and wants)

- ◆ Maintain but manage power (don't let their power turn into arrogance)

- ◆ Focus on their responsibilities

And, remember, it is moral courage that determines the standard of leadership in the practical arenas of politics, business, academics, and the community.

Be kind; for everyone is having a hard battle.
—Plato

Run Your Own Race

I hope that what I have shared in this book will inspire you to compete with confidence, to lead with vision, to follow your own path with honesty, dignity, and integrity.

As I mentioned above, what I propose women must do to forever break out of their artificially imposed limitations will take courage. There will be times that they will have to fight against the good-old-boy network, or turn the other cheek against outrageous slings and arrows, or overcome the seemingly ever-present stereotyping of women in general, and ambitious women in particular.

When you find the going to be tough, you might reflect on what Kierkegaard, Nietzsche, Camus, and Sartre, all great observers of human nature, each proclaimed to be true — that courage is not the absence of despair, but rather the capacity to move ahead in spite of despair. The word "courage" comes from the French word "coeur," meaning "heart," which I believe is an important element of leadership to remember. Successful women leaders will have the capacity

to lead not just with their head, but also with their heart —
an innovative and winning combination.

In closing, let me give you one more challenge. As you
make your way to the top, why not take someone with you?
When you mentor and encourage other women like yourself, you help open the doors for all of us and create a future
of unlimited possibilities for our daughters, granddaughters,
and all who follow.

To the women of America, I wish you complete
success.

About the Author

Linda Wheeler, a public speaker and author, is the founder and president of Phoenix Rising 2000, a leadership and management consulting firm. She holds a Masters in Public Administration from the John F. Kennedy School of Government at Harvard University. Linda achieved certificates of leadership training from the University of Washington, Duke University, and again, the renowned Kennedy School of Government. Linda lives in Olympia, Washington, with her husband, James, and their daughter, Jamielyn.

References & Additional Reading

Cantor, Dorothy W., Toni Bernay, with Jean Stoess. *Women In Power: The Secrets of Leadership.* Houghton Mifflin Company, 1992.

Colón, Rafael. *Journey To Success: 8 Steps to Avoid the Career Dormido Virus.* Voices Internacional, 1998.

Heifetz, Ronald A. *Leadership Without Easy Answers.* Harvard University Press, 1996.

May, Rollo. *The Courage to Create.* W. W. Norton and Company, 1994.

Rost, Joseph C. *Leadership For The Twenty First Century.* Praeger Publisher, 1993.

Tracy, Laura. *Competition Among Women: The Secret Between Us.* Little Brown & Company, 1991.

Order Form

Qty.	Title	Price	Total
	The Executive Alley	$9.95	
Shipping and Handling Add $3.50 for orders in the US / Add $7.50 for Global Priority			
Sales tax (WA state residents only, add 8.6%)			
Total Enclosed			

Telephone orders:
Call 1-800-461-1931
Have your VISA or
MasterCard ready.

INTL. telephone orders:
Toll free 1-877-250-5500
Have your credit card ready.

Fax orders:
425-672-8597
Fill out this order form and fax.

Postal orders:
Hara Publishing
P.O. Box 19732
Seattle, WA 98109

E-mail orders:
harapub@foxinternet.net

Method of Payment:

☐ [check image] Check or Money Order

☐ VISA

☐ MasterCard

Expiration Date: _____

Card #: _____

Signature: _____

_____

Name: _____

Address: _____

City: _____ State: _____ Zip: _____

Daytime Phone: (   ) _____

Quantity discounts are available.
Call (425) 398-3679 for more information.
Thank you for your order!